NUGGETS FOR MAGNETING GLOBAL MONEY

Through eBook Creation and Self Publishing

TOYOSI ADE-ABASS

TOYOSI ADE-ABASS

Cover design by: Art Painter
Library of Congress Control Number: 2018675309
Printed in the United States of America

DEDICATION
I dedicate this book to the Lord God Almighty for making
it possible for me to write this book successfully.

CONTENTS

Title Page

Copyright

Dedication

Introduction

NUGGETS FOR MAGNETING GLOBAL MONEY   1

Toyosi Ade-Abass   2

CHAPTER 1   3

This book is not: 4

What is the book really about and what do you stand to benefit?   5

CHAPTER 2   7

CHAPTER 3   8

PUBLISHING   10

TYPES OF WRITING   11

CHAPTER 4   13

PURPOSEFUL WRITING   15

CHAPTER 5   17

GUIDES TO WRITING A BESTSELLER   18

CHAPTER 6   20

CHARACTERISTICS OF E-books   21

BENEFITS OF E-books   23

HOW TO MAKE AN E-book   24

CHAPTER 7   25

PREPARING YOUR EBOOK WITH MS WORD   26

NOTE   29

CHAPTER 8   30

CHAPTER 9   33

ADVANCED FORMATTING   35

The steps for using the Kindle Create are as follows: 36

CHAPTER 10   38

STEP BY STEP ON HOW TO GENERATE FREE ISBN FOR YOUR BOOK FROM YOUR AMAZON ACCOUNT   39

NOTE: 40

CHAPTER 11   41

HOW TO BE SUCCESSFUL TRAINING OTHERS   43

CHAPTER 12   44

I'd forward this response to you for records purposes   48

KDP would credit any account you provide.   49

Go to payoneer to apply.   50

CHAPTER 13   51

CHAPTER 14   52

MEN LIKE MONEY, SO WHY DOES IT IRRITATES THEM?   53

THE RICH FOOL   54

Now you can identify, the rich fool, what about the poor idiot?   55

JOURNEYING TOWARDS WRECKAGE   56

THE RECOMMENDED PATH   57

THE MISSING GOAT NO 3   58

Have a blessed day....!!!   60

Enjoy life with what you have and who you are.   61

Washing and thinking   62

- YOU MAY BE PROMoTED   63

What about you?   64

The story begins   65

the man looked at the disciple and replied with a smile   69

    71

About The Author   73

INTRODUCTION

This book "Nuggets for Magnecting Global Money" is a book truly inspired to meet the needs of those who are tired of being oppressed, suppressed and reduced by their environments. It is further written for those who are ready to put their failure between them and reach out to the world with their skill, thereby, magneting global money. it must be clearly understood that we are in a generation where nothing good comes easy and goes for nothing. Many people are busy running money only few people are in search of what money will run after. Empty men don't riches only men of value do. In this book, you would learn how to add value to yourself, you will learn how to take advantage of this time and season. We are in a digital world, and the whole world seems to be compact because of the power of networking. I remember in time past whenever I am broke I will cry unto God in prayers to bless me, but to my amusement, the Lord will give ideas instead of money. It took time for me to realise that God wanted me to convert the ideas into monetary value. Are you in this category? Do you have ideas that you want to send to the world? You can put it into writing. In this book, you will learn how to delevop your writing skills so that it can be accepted globally. This book will help you in e-book creation and publishing.

After reading this book and following the principles that will be learnt, I have no doubt that your life will begin to magnet money globally.

NUGGETS FOR MAGNETING GLOBAL MONEY

(A guide to Creative writing and Self-Publishing)

TOYOSI ADE-ABASS

CHAPTER 1
WHAT THIS BOOK IS NOT ABOUT

There are some myths which needs to be clarified which have been running through the mind of most people. Through the consistent use of your writing skills you will begin to earn steadily.

THIS BOOK IS NOT:

- a get-rich-quick scheme
- a book that will exploit you of your precious time or hard earned money/resources.
- a multi-level marketing book or networking book.
- a book where you write alone and not publish online.

WHAT IS THE BOOK REALLY ABOUT AND WHAT DO YOU STAND TO BENEFIT?

Here are the five fundamental benefits and gains you will derive from this book:

- ✓ You will learn the Basic Method of eBook Creation and Publishing.
- ✓ You will learn how to open your KDP Amazon Account at no cost.
- ✓ You will learn how to publish your book using your KDP account.
- ✓ You will learn how to write a strong and purposeful book and become a potential bestseller.
- ✓ You will learn how to go to KDP to publish your eBooks the basic way.

This book is not only good and recommended for beginners, but also for experienced writers. It will also serve as a major requirement and the only foundation needed to have access to the Advanced Method of Publishing which will eventually lead you to becoming a professional and certified

writer.

CHAPTER 2

HISTORY OF WRITING

Before going into details of what writing is all about, let us quickly make a few comments (review) on the history of the book. It's origin and how it all started.

This book was originally a parchment, a rolled manuscript made from the papyrus plant. The Romans developed the manuscript which was made of wood and animal skins, opened like a book and had actual pages.

The first book in Mass production is the Gutenberg Bible. So Johannes Gutenberg invented the Book. It's said that the first real paper book was made in China.

It's made from large pulp made of blackberries, hemp, bark and even fish, which can be pressed and dried into paper. Each piece of paper is about the size of a newspaper and it's called "a piece of paper".

CHAPTER 3

RUDIMENTS OF WRITING AND PUBLISHING

WHAT IS WRITING?

Writing is an art of expressing thought and knowledge, which can turn your skills high(improve).

The art of writing is the" art of discovering what you believe." That insightful perspective was articulated by the great author Gustav Flaubert. And it captures my experience well.

I often get new ideas when meditating or sometimes during conversation. Writing, at its best, is a form of thinking. It clarifies our thoughts. And it leads to new thoughts. It even expands us, when it's done right.

When we write, we discover, we deepen our understanding, and we remember better. In setting goals, it can be very beneficial to write them out, and chart out the intermediate and more immediate steps that it will take to reach the goal. It stimulates new thought. And it generates motivation.

Writing is not restricted to a set of people, race, language or colour. Anyone can choose to write and become a billionaire earning in dollars and pounds through this skill.

Writing goes farther than where the two legs of the writer could possibly get to. So, through your writing, your message(s) can get to the ends of the earth making a global impact. It can as well create a huge traffic of followers for you around the globe thereby having more people believing in your cause and convictions.Your book(s) makes you an authority and a Voice wherever you find yourself.

A Book is a legacy that outlives the writer. It also and always serves as a blessing to its readers. It also proffers solutions to generations all over the universe long after your death.

PUBLISHING

In writing for publication, the question to ask is what are your set goals? What do you aim to achieve?
All these determines what you write and your purpose of writing.

TYPES OF WRITING

There are different types of writing styles which are:

- Narrative writing
- Descriptive writing
- Persuasive writing
- Expository writing
- Creative writing
- Objective writing
- Subjective writing
- Review writing
- Technical writing
- Poetic writing and so on.

All the types of writing can be grouped under four(4) headings namely: Narrative, Descriptive, Persuasive and Expoisitory.

1. Narrative Writing

This is the most basic form of storytelling and it shares something that happens to a character. It is most times mistaken as descriptive writing, not all narratives are very detailed. It can be found in poetry, novels and short stories. It have a habit of putting riders into a state of imagination. A good narrative has a flow in it's events.

2. Descriptive Writing

This involves capturing every detail of what you are writing about; the place, person or scene. It also create an explicit image in the readers mind. This writing connects with the readers by appealing to their senses. It employ literary devices such as metaphors to engage their audience(readers). Examples are fictional novels.

3. Persuasive Writing

This is about getting your point across and trying to convince the reader of your idea or thoughts. It includes the writer's opinion, with the writer providing reasons, evidence and justification to back up their claims. Examples of articles with persuasive writing are Argumentative essays for academic papers. While writing, the writer has to make sure he stands his ground and secure the point he is trying to make. A good persuasive writing is not equivocal.

4. Expository Writing

This tries to answer any questions a reader might have; the writer should make it as clear as possible and avoid technical jargon. Expository writing provides evidence (proof), statistics (results) and focus on a certain topic. This type of writing is not meant to express the writer's opinion or ideas, it's all about proven facts. Examples are scientific writings, textbooks etc.

CHAPTER 4

STRONG WRITING AND PURPOSEFUL WRITING

STRONG WRITING

This is the writing that is captivating right from start. It is the writing that captures the attention of the reader as a result of the style, language, imagery, and rhetoric employed right from the start and holds him bound until he finished reading the whole book(suspense). Such stir up the curiosity of the reader keeps him yearning for more until the very end of the story.

In another definition, strong writing should also meet the needs of your target audience, to the extent that they would be willing to pay for it or do anything to have your work. This simply means that a book should be targeted to solve a problem. People will pay a very high price for the knowledge they need to have their problems solved.

Characteristics of a Strong Writing

1. It is readable: a readable work is grammatically sound. It may not always be grammatically right, but does not have punctuations getting in the way of significance.

2. It is tangible: a writing that has its contents relatable to real world ways which can be easily approachable by the reader is a strong writing.

3. It is concentrated, driving it's reader towards the aim of which it is written.

4. It must be growing, flowing and graceful with no missing information which can make the reader

stumble.

5. It is full of enthusiasm.

6. It must be well suited for it's audience: understanding your audience, the knowledge they hold, the languages they speak and their beliefs make your writing a strong one.

Qualities of Strong Writing

❖ **FOCUS**

A strong writing has a single clear central idea and is not vague.

❖ **UNITY**

All parts and chapters of a strong writing relate to the main idea.

❖ **COHERENCE**

A strong writing should be orderly, reasonable and possess a notable amount of consistency. Everything should make sense to the reader.

❖ **DEVELOPMENT**

A strong writing has ideas explained and illustrated through examples, details and description.

❖ **ACCURACY**

There should be a good level of correctness in the grammar used in writing, as incorrect grammar can be a turn-off to your reader.

Some other traits of writing include: ideas, word choice, fluency of sentences, conventions.

PURPOSEFUL WRITING

A purposeful writing is a writing that achieve a goal (what the writer wants to talk about) and satisfy the desire (what the writer wants the readers to know about what he want to talk about) of the reader.

What is purpose?

Purpose:- is something set up as an object or end to be attained.

Intention:- is writing with determination, intention, and meaning. It also means writing with a goal in mind - Complete determination to meet your goal. So we see that writing must have purpose and intention.

The four(4) core purpose for a writing include:

- ☐ To inform
- ☐ To entertain
- ☐ To persuade
- ☐ To express feelings.

Others which can be grouped under the four(4) core purposes are to:

- ➢ describe
- ➢ learn/explore
- ➢ explain
- ➢ evaluate
- ➢ argue
- ➢ meditate
- ➢ solve problems.

Note

Audience in terms of writing is a group of readers who read a particular piece of writing.To achieve a strong and purposeful writing, you need to determine the type of audience you are writing to or for in order to write effectively.

CHAPTER 5

BESTSELLERS

When we say a BESTSELLER, we are referring to a book or a publication that has the highest number of sold-out copies in relation to other books in its category within a given time frame.

A bestseller:- is an author who has written and published many books that are recognized worldwide. Below is a list of all-time bestsellers with quantities sold.

- ✓ Da Vinci Code by Dan Brown. 5,094,805 in sales.
- ✓ Harry Potter and the Deathly Hallows by J.K Rowling 4,475,152 in sales.
- ✓ Harry Potter and the Philosopher's Stone by J.K Rowling 4,200,654 in sales.
- ✓ The Lord of the rings by J.R.R Tolkien
- ✓ A tale of two cities by Charles Dickens
- ✓ The adventure of Pinocchio by Carlo Collodi
- ✓ The Lion, the witch and the wardrobe by C.S. Lewis.

GUIDES TO WRITING A BESTSELLER

Here are some hints for writing a bestseller:

- ➤ Start with a big idea. Something fresh and interesting. You must find an idea that will get readers excited to pick up your book. A small idea for a book results in small sales.

- ➤ Start immediately because others may have similar idea. No procrastination!

- ➤ Write with the audience in mind. Bestsellers are sticky. The book needs to be written in a way where it can be easily shared and talked about, because it touches on some universal theme. Stephen King says you write the first draft with the door closed and the second draft with the door open.

- ➤ Edit for clarity, not perfection. Bestsellers are clear. Take out all the clutter that distracts your reader from the true message.

- ➤ Package your book to spread. Bestsellers are packaged to sell. The title, cover, and design are all optimized to help the message spread.

- ➤ Never stop launching. Bestsellers are perennial.

- ➤ Never stop trying but keep pushing. The bestselling books of all time typically didn't come out the gates as immediate successes. But because of their timeless nature, they just kept selling.

LET'S DIGRESS A BIT

Jeff Bezos (born 1964) is the founder and executive chairman of Amazon. With a net worth of more than $200 billion, he was once the richest man in the world according to Forbes and Bloomberg billionaire index (June 2021).

When 16-year-old Jeff got a summer job frying up burgers at

McDonald's in 1980, he learned all he could from the experience He was a cook, and they wouldn't let him anywhere near the customers As a grill man, the most challenging thing for Bezos "was keeping everything going at the right pace during a rush The experience was Bezos' first hands-on brush with retail He spent the summer studying the company's automation improvements, like beeps and signals for when to scramble his eggs, flip his burgers, and pull his fries out of the boiling vat. The job also gave him early insight into customer service Today, "customer obsession" is the first one of Amazon's leadership principles. As for Bezos's time at McDonald's, his advice for young people is to always keep your eyes open for lessons to learn at any gig, even it's just flipping burgers. "You can learn responsibility in any job, if you take it seriously," "You learn a lot as a teenager working at McDonald's," he said. "It's different from what you learn in school. Don't underestimate the value of that!"

CHAPTER 6
INTRODUCTION TO E-BOOK

An e-book or eBook also know as an electronic book is a book publication made in digital format that can be downloaded making it readable on the flat panel display of a compatible device such as a computer, laptop, smart phone or tablet consisting of text, images, or both. Several books that are available in printed versions can be found as ebooks. This include everything from best-selling fiction, classics to reference and academic texts.

E-Books are generally cheaper than paper books and allow you to store hundreds of books on one device at the touch of a button.

It is high time we broadened our minds! Go for what works in order to remain relevant... It has become an electronic world.

CHARACTERISTICS OF E-BOOKS

There are certain characteristics that differentiate an ebook from other files that can be read on digital devices such as:

- An eBook is a non-editable book presented in a digital format - an electronic book.

- No matter the size of the device used, it is a read only document that can fit into any screen. The formatted texts, chapters, line breaks and images of the book will always resize to fit the device you are reading on.

- An ebook with it's reflowable text provides a much better reading experience.

E-READERS

An e-reader, also called an e-book reader or e-book device, is a mobile electronic device that is designed primarily for the purpose of storing and reading digital e-books and periodicals.

Any device that can display text on a screen may act as an e-reader; however, specialized e-reader devices may optimize portability, readability, and battery life for this purpose. Their main advantage over printed books is portability. This is because an e-reader is capable of holding thousands of books while weighing less than one book, and the convenience provided due to add-on features.

A major e-reader series designed by AMAZON is the 'Amazon Kindle' which allow readers to browse, buy, download and read ebooks, magazines, newspapers and other digital media via wireless networking to the Kindle Store.

E-BOOK FORMAT

There are top five (5) ebook formats which include EPUB, AZW, MOBI, TXT, PDF.

- ❖ **EPUB**

An EPUB, or electronic publication, is the most widely supported eBook format and can be read on a variety of devices, including computers, smartphones, tablets, and most eReaders (except Kindles). EPUB was created by the International Digital Publishing Forum(IDPF).

❖ **AZW (.azw)**

AZW files, also known as Kindle files, were developed by Amazon for its Kindle eReaders, Additively, they are only accessible from the Amazon online bookstore. These files can store complex content like bookmarks, annotations, and highlights.

❖ **MOBI (.mobi)**

This is a format designed for PDAs (Personal Digital Assistants) and other mobile devices. It can also be used on the Kindle.

❖ **TXT (.txt)**

A plain text file is the simplest file format that uses the file extension .txt. These files are used strictly for text, images and graphs are not supported. Because of their simplicity, these files are usually for storing information with no formatting beyond basic fonts and font styles. TXT files are great for text-heavy eBooks, like research reports.

❖ **PDF (.pdf)**

A PDF, also known as a Portable Document Format, it doesn't have a characteristics of an eBook because it's not reflowable. It's a format most people are familiar. The PDF format was created by Adobe.

Common places where eBooks can be found include

☐ Amazon

☐ Barnes and Noble

☐ Google Play

☐ Apple Books.

Why create an e-Book?

✓ Self-publishing purpose

✓ As part of marketing strategy

BENEFITS OF E-BOOKS

The aim of ebook is to simplify and enhance the overall learning experience.

1) Ebooks occupy less space.

2) They can be easily updated.

3) The contents of ebooks can be shared with multiple users at once.

4) Electronic books are cheap and affordable.

5) They can be downloaded instantly.

6) The font size can be changed.

7) Ebooks can easily be searched.

HOW TO MAKE AN E-BOOK

Define your objective-why are you writing the book and who are you writing it for. (This will help you choose a title).

Outline the book into an introduction, chapters and possibly call to action.

Writing the eBook Include details and be creative (note that some eBooks have low content, like colouring books and planners).

When you are done writing, proofread.

Convert (upload), publish, and promote the eBook.

CHAPTER 7

MICROSOFT WORD AND ITs USEFULNESS

Microsoft Word is a word document/app where you type whatever work you have put into writing.

There are other word processing apps, like WPS, Pages from Apple, Google Docs etc.

BUT .... Amazon KDP, works well with Microsoft Word.

PREPARING YOUR EBOOK WITH MS WORD

Please, give your lesson note manuscript a unique title.

Now we'll talk about the content and arrangement of a book

Some sections and segments of your book to be converted to eBook, or for normal publication include:

- ☐ Cover page
- ☐ Copyright page
- ☐ Dedication
- ☐ Acknowledgements
- ☐ Table of contents (ToC)
- ☐ Introduction
- ☐ Body (or Chapters)
- ☐ Back page (blurb/About the author)

- ❖ **Cover page:-** That is the first thing you see of a book. For you to have a good book, all the above listed must be there.

- ❖ **Copyright© page:-** That's the protection ownership rights to the contents of the book.

NOTE:

The information written in any book in the copyright pages, tells you the extent to which you can use the contents and who to contact before usage. Copyright abuse is a crime. It can cost you money and your freedom – imprisonment. Some of the books you buy in our streets/ bookshops in Africa are written by foreigners. If you take them out of the country, you could get into trouble because most are pirated copies. The developed countries of the world take this very seriously.

❖ Dedication Page

This is where the author mentions the names of people their book is dedicated to and why.

❖ Acknowledgement Page

The author uses this section to express gratitude towards the people that contributed to the production of the book.

❖ Table of Contents (ToC)

This is a list of chapter headings and the page numbers where they begin. It could also list major sections that it contains.

❖ Introduction

This gives you an overview of the book, what the subject matter is, so that you have a general idea before you go into the book You should only conclude the introduction when you are done with the whole write up. It gives a complete picture of all that is in the book in a nutshell. So you may start your introduction, have a draft of it, but finish it when you have the complete picture of what you're writing.

❖ Chapters

This is where the plot is laid out, your story is told, and your reader is mesmerized. This is what the whole book is about, and your content should be split up logically so that it's easy to follow and keep track. This works hand in hand with your table of contents. What you are writing about will determine whether you need a conclusion, final thoughts or just a good ending to your story.

❖ Back Page

Here you should have a blurb (short piece that describes what the book is about) and a brief summary about the author. This could be their previous work, education, personal life etc.

However, note that the order above isn't sacrosanct. Also there are other sections a book can have but we won't go into those ones.

NOTE:

Poems and other forms of writing have their own layout.

So for this exercise, aim at *26* to *28* pages Please when writing your notes, add some flesh to it. The minimum number of pages to publish on Amazon is *24. It must not be less than 24 pages.

There are more people looking for who to publish for them than those who know how to. Which side do you belong? So if you can sit down and get through this... That could be an additional stream of income.

There are three types of Books

- eBook

- Paperback

- Hardcopy

In this basic class, we are looking at only e-book. The specifications for paperback and hardcover are different. eBook is MUCH simpler than paperback .

NOTE

Any publication can be done in the 3

- ➢ **Paperback:-** are physical books with soft cover that can be printed.
- ➢ **Hardcopy:-** is physical book with hard cover.

CHAPTER 8
FORMATTING YOUR E-BOOK WITH A CUSTOMIZED TEMPLATE

WHAT IS FORMATTING?

Formatting is the arrangement of your stored data in a special and specified style.

The formatting of your book determines how your book will look like, the main reason the set rules and standard need to be followed.

Note: Your book will not be accepted on the Amazon Kindle if it is not well formatted.

Standard formatting for eBooks feature a dynamic, re-flowable layout for text and images to make sure your eBook looks great when viewed on every size and shape eReader, mobile device and tablet.

Today's readers hold their eBooks to the same standards as printed books, making it more important than ever to showcase a professionalism with your eBook that translates across any popular mobile device or eReader, like the Kindle.

TEMPLATE

A template is a pre-formatted file type that can be used to quickly create a specific file. Everything such as font, size, color and background pictures are pre-formatted but users can also edit them. Template also refer to resource where already prepared samples is presented.

When writing your manuscript, you can either use a customized template (it could be yours or someone else's) or create a new format while you write with the flow.

Steps in Formatting

Open the template.
Don't tamper with the settings.
Just DELETE the content of each page.
Copy your own from your manuscript.
Paste on the template

Very very simple

For example,

Delete INTRODUCTION page on the createspace template, copy your own and paste. That's all.

Using a customized template to format your eBook, the basic template for use is the "CreateSpae Template". Copy and paste your manuscript into this template or begin typing. Before using the template, remove any existing text. The book can be divided into the following:

- Title
- Author name
- Copyright
- Acknowledgement
- Contents
- Chapters
- About the Author.

For formatting in the basic level:

- When you open the word document.

- Click on Format>>Document>>Margins (For Mac, may be slightly different for Windows).

- The specifications on the margin:

☐ Top: 0.76"

☐ Left: 0.76"

☐ Gutter: 0.14"

☐ Bottom: 0.76"

☐ Right: 0.6"

☐ Gutter position: Left

- Set Page numbers in the footer.

- Set Title of the book as the header.

Note:

This is a manual form of formatting manuscript. If your formatting is poor, KDP Amazon will not process it.

CHAPTER 9
CREATING YOUR KDP ACCOUNT ON AMAZON

You need to have an account on the Amazon Kindle Direct Publishing space for you to be able to publish your books. Here are step by step guides on how to create your KDP account on Amazon:

1. Open your browser.
2. In the search box type "kdp.amazon.com".
3. A home page will open up with an animation of a man the table.
4. Click on SIGN UP.
5. Fill in your first and last name, your email address and your password.
6. Crosscheck your details to be sure you filled the correct details.
7. When you are sure you have typed the right information, click on **create your kdp account.** An email will be sent to you asking you to verify your account.
8. Use the link in the email you have received to verify your account.
9. An OTP (One Time Password) will be sent to you.
10. Input the code sent to you in the box provided for it. Once the code is confirmed, you will be taken to another page with a form to be filled.
11. Fill in your details, following the instructions on your screen. Where you see postal code, pls Google your local govt code (the place you reside.) and fill it there.

12. Fill in the tax verification form.
13. Fill in the other necessary information.
14. Submit, you are done.

Note:

For more guidance, feel free to watch tutorial videos on YouTube.

ADVANCED FORMATTING

This style is more professional than the basic style (previous chapter). This advanced method transforms your book using an application called the KINDLE CREATE App.

THE STEPS FOR USING THE KINDLE CREATE ARE AS FOLLOWS:

1. Download the Kindle Create App from Amazon's KDP store.
2. Install the application on a Window 64-bit PC.
3. Run the application.
4. Select the unformatted document from your computer to import it.
5. Fill out the front and back matter with the necessary information.
6. Choose a theme to style the manuscript.
7. Place the cursor on Chapter One.
8. Click Insert and Table of Contents to generate the table of contents.
9. Highlight and style the first paragraph, then repeat for the remaining ones.
10. Save the manuscript in the kdf package.
11. Examine and publish the eBook.

Editing the CreateSpace Template:
Highlight what you want to change and replace with your own content. Ensure you maintain the formatting of the template.

➢ Book Title
➢ Author Name
➢ Copyright details
➢ ISBN(if you have one)
➢ Dedication
➢ Table of Contents (see below)

- ➤ Acknowledgements
- ➤ Chapter Headings and Content (see below)
- ➤ Update the header on page 1 (chapter 1), it's an Odd Page Header.
- ➤ Enter the book title
- ➤ Uncheck different first page
- ➤ Select different Odd and Even pages
- ➤ Update the header on page 2 (chapter 1), it is an Even Page Header.
- ➤ Enter the Author name
- ➤ Update the chapters
- ➤ Replace Chapter Name place holders with your chapter names
- ➤ Paste the content for each chapter maintaining the document format.
- ➤ Delete the chapters you do not need

Once you have pasted all the chapters, update the Table of Contents page numbers to the actual page number of each chapter. Update about the Author content with your own information. Proofread, correct and save your document.

CHAPTER 10

INTERNATIONAL STANDARD BOOK NUMBER (ISBN)

ISBN is a national and international standard identification number for uniquely identifying books, i.e. publications that are not intended to continue indefinitely.

STEP BY STEP ON HOW TO GENERATE FREE ISBN FOR YOUR BOOK FROM YOUR AMAZON ACCOUNT

- ✓ Log on to kdp account.
- ✓ Go to bookshelf and start the paper back process.
- ✓ Continue the process until you get to the point where you will see the ISBN information. It will ask you if you want the kdp ISBN or not. So you click it and wait for your ISBN.

NOTE:

You must always get your ISBN ready before publishing any book particularly when working on international standard books.

CHAPTER 11

MEANS OF EARNING MONEY THROUGH THE ACQUIRED SKILLS

There are three (3) majors means of making money through this skill. They are through:
- ➢ Earning Royalties through your self published books.
- ➢ Consultancy
- ➢ Monetization Exercise

❖ ROYALTIES

These are the money percentage gotten when your self published books are sold and purchased.
When you earn royalties, they reflect on the **royalties' dashboard.**

❖ CONSULTANCY

An Amazon kdp consultant is one who:
- helps people publish their books.
- guides other publishers on the steps to take while creating their books.
- you reach out to when encountering difficulties in creating and publishing your ebooks or paperbacks.

Being a consultant is another way to earn money in this Amazon kdp space.

❖ MONETIZATION EXERCISE

This is the practical method of making money which is referred to as Training the Trainer. It has nothing to do with Amazon but has to do with the management of WRITE-FOR-ME organization. Been connected to the organization is life changing. You make money here when you help other people to acquire this same skill that you have acquired.

You organize a basic online ebook training for them. You can use WhatsApp or Telegram as a platform to train them.

After creating the training platform using either of the means mentioned earlier, generate an invite link, use it to invite people on different social media platforms, make the invitation general as you don't know who may be interested.

HOW TO BE SUCCESSFUL TRAINING OTHERS

This include:
- ❖ Give a brief and true profile of who you truly are.
- ❖ Make sure you start the class with excitement.
- ❖ Make sure you are passionate in your teaching.
- ❖ Ensure that you monitor those responding to your teachings and those who are not.
- ❖ As the training continues commend those who are flowing with you and do not hesitate to make comments on those who are not serious with the training and do it without apology.
- ❖ Make sure that you also keep the scheduled time as the leader.
- ❖ Make sure you are well prepared for each class.
- ❖ Know that if you beg them to come to class, you will also beg them to stay and learn. So do not beg anyone to come to class.
- ❖ Remove anyone who is not showing seriousness after you've carefully observed the person, to maintain the orderliness of the class.
- ❖ Do not allow anyone post anything outside the context of the class either religion information or otherwise.
- ❖ Lastly, keep an intimate relationship and trust in God for optimum output.

CHAPTER 12

CREATING YOUR PAYONEER ACCOUNT

PAYONEER is the bank preferred among many Foreign authors who are not United State resident.

SIGN PROCESS
- Open your browser, perhaps Google.
- Type the payoneer.com link
- Use the Google payoneer sign up.
- Sign up with your email address, create a password, verify your email address and fill out all the necessary.
- Required details such as name, ID or passport number, residential address.

Country of residence and banking details
1) Type www.payoneer.com on your browser.
2) Click register.
3)   Select the appropriate option from the drop-down box (individual or another you prefer).
4)   then select "get paid by international clients or market places".
5) Then click register.

for the interface fill in the following:
1) Name
2) Surname
3) Email address
4) Re-enter Email address
5) Date of birth
6) Then click next

For second, the next interface fill in the following details:
1) Country of residence
2) Address
3) Zip code (search the net for zip code of where you reside).
4) Mobile Number
5) Verification Code sent to your mobile number.

For the third interface, fill in the following details:
1) Your email address
2) Your password
3) Re-enter password
4) Choose your security questions and answers.
5) Your ID or passport number.
For the fourth and final interface, fill in the following details:
1) Your bank name
2) Your bank number
3) Indicate if it is a cheque or savings
4) Swift code
5) And your registration is done.

Wait for approval of your account
After your account has been approved:
- Go to your homepage.
- Click on receive payments.
- Click on global payments.
- For receiving in dollar options click on USD option, for receiving in pounds click in the UK auction.

(To avoid challenges, we will use the US located account, it will give you a first century bank account domiciled in the US this account is only accepted accepted by the Amazon KDP).
Once created, click on the USD option to capture the bank details that will be uploaded to Kindle Direct publishing are the following:
1) Bank Name
2) Band Address

3) Routing (ABA)
4) Account Number Domiciled
5) Account Type
6) Beneficiary Name

NOTE:

- THE USE OF PAYONEER ACCOUNT IS OPTIONAL IF YOU HAVE OTHER ACCOUNTS ACCEPTABLE TO KDP. FOR EXAMPLE PAYPAL.

- ON WITHDRAWING FROM PAYONEER:

Your best bet is to apply for the ATM card and you can withdraw on the go. Read up from their site how to apply.

- PAYONEER IS A COMPANY ON IT'S OWN AND HAS NO OFFICIAL BUSINESS RELATIONSHIP WITH KDP/AMAZON - THEY OFFER ONLINE PAYMENT SERVICES.

- ON FIXING YOUR PAYONEER ACCOUNT TO KDP

Login in to your kdp account....... Click on 'Your Account' at the topmost part, where you have English, Help, Sign Out. It will open a space for you with the caption 'Author/Publisher Information' move down, you would see what you are looking for. There, you can add your bank with the USA account already generated on Payoneer.... I hope you would find this helpful..........Good luck. PLEASE NOTE: If you click on your account, kdp may require that you put a one time password (OTP) that they would send to you before you could access your account.... Please put it and continue......It is that simple.

- PAYONEER ID VERSUS PAYONEER'S BANK ACCOUNT

Your payoneer ID is different from your allocated bank account. You get a payoneer ID upon registration and a bank account after you apply and it's approved.

- OPENING OR NOT OPENING YOUR PAYONEER ACCOUNT HAS NOTHING TO DO WITH YOUR PUBLISHING AND GRADUATING WITH DISTINCTION

Payoneer and Kdp has no working relationship. Payoneer is only an online banking system to allow digital sellers get their money.

On the other hand, Kdp only expects you to provide a workable account or opt for cheque.

So if you're having issues with payoneer, opt for cheque payment from kdp.

I'D FORWARD THIS RESPONSE TO YOU FOR RECORDS PURPOSES

- IT IS NOT COMPULSORY TO OPEN A PAYONEER ACCOUNT AND IT CANNOT STOP YOUR PUBLISHING PROGRESS

- CASHING OUT FROM KDP

Cheque or transfer.

Cheque: they'd send you a physical cheque tons designated address.

Transfer: the reason you created a payoneer account or you can get a friend or relations with a US based account to use.

KDP WOULD CREDIT ANY ACCOUNT YOU PROVIDE.

Remember, with your payoneer account, you can request for an ATM card, which you can use to cash your money from any ATM. Read up from payoneer to request for one.

GO TO PAYONEER TO APPLY.

Please don't rush o...

- ON PAYONEER'S OTP NOT GETTING TO YOU ON TIME

If you request for SMS and it doesn't deliver on time, opt for a phone call - that would come almost immediately. Because it's delivery is timed and when that time elapses, it'd expire.

- THE DIGITAL WORLD IS A FAST PACED ENVIRONMENT

-

CHAPTER 13
CREATING YOUR COVER PAGE, UPLOADING AND PUBLISHING YOUR E-BOOK

Now to begin publishing after editing your work using the customized template you come to KDP account and click on Kindle eBook as indicated above.

When you are done formatting your manuscript, save it, the next step is to upload it..

- ➤ Sign in into your KDP account through kdp.amazon.com.
- ➤ Near the top of the homepage, you will find Bookshelf. Click on that.
- ➤ Click on kindle   eBook on the left.
  - • It will take you through three forms   before you upload.
  - • On the first form, you will enter the book details.
  - • On the second form, you will.
- ➤ Upload your manuscript (pick it where you saved it).
- ➤ Create your cover.
- ➤ Preview your ebook

The final form focuses on Pricing and Distribution.

Once everything is complete select *Save and Publish* and you are done.

CHAPTER 14

LIFE LESSONS

THE RICH FOOL & THE POOR IDIOT

These are frightening description, not when my good friend, Joe Agbro, a seasoned journalist recently posted quoting Albert Camus, that, *"It's a kind of spiritual snobbery that makes people think they can be happy without money."* How correct or wrong isn't my concern, as much as it aligns with the saying of the wisest and richest man whoever lived, besides Jesus Christ - Solomon Jesse, I quote; *"money is the answer to everything."* (Ecc. 10:19).

MENTIONING MONEY IRRITATES AN AVERAGE MAN, YET.....

No fewer than majority who started reading this post would have quitted the moment I mentioned money. And those still reading, majorly are already irritated. I doubt if up to 25% of those who saw and started to read this charger (changer), would read to the end.

Strangely, what irritates most men, they are actually in love with it, no wonder, the next popular quote to that of King Solomon Jesse, was made by brother Paul when he said; *"the love of money is the root of all evil"* (1Timothy 6:10).

MEN LIKE MONEY, SO WHY DOES IT IRRITATES THEM?

The lack of money and the torment of that lack had taken most men through, makes them to adopt the outward concept to disdain and be irritated by the mere mentioning of money. And to crown their failings, they painfully, find themselves hating and disdaining those in possession of money.

Somehow, those in possession of money, wouldn't help matters too, as they intentionally live the bigger than life, lifestyle backed by swelling arrogance, a decent into idolizing money.

The aforementioned, is the background to this treatise, *THE RICH FOOL AND POOR IDIOT*. If you're still reading, I'd be shocked if you continue to the end. Notwithstanding, I'd continue to finish my part of this business, which is to liberate you.

THE RICH FOOL

My Mentor told the next story to elaborate, who the rich fool was and is. He said;
"The ground of a certain rich man yielded an abundant harvest. He thought to himself, 'What shall I do? I have no place to store my crops.'

"Then he said, 'This is what I'll do. I will tear down my barns and build bigger ones, and there I will store my surplus grain. And I'll say to myself, "You have plenty of grain laid up for many years. Take life easy; eat, drink and be merry. But God said to him, 'You fool! This very night your life will be demanded from you.Then who will get what you have prepared for yourself?'
"This is how it will be with whoever stores up things for themselves but is not rich toward God." (Luke 12:16-21).

Hope you read that, the rich man bereft of character and Godliness, is classified here as a fool. Such people become so rich to discredit the existence of God and so are promoters of all manners of ungodliness and anything that goes against the will of God. David Jesse, the father to Solomon Jesse, said; *"The fool says in his heart, "There is no God."* (Psalm 14:1).

NOW YOU CAN IDENTIFY, THE RICH FOOL, WHAT ABOUT THE POOR IDIOT?

THE POOR IDIOT

Is that man or woman who relishes in poverty and discards anything that will liberate them. Unlike the rich fool, the poor idiot lives in contrast daily hoping and wishing for money, besides a dying love for money, yet unconsciously disdaining money and doing nothing to make money. Desiring the dainty of the rich, yet ignoring the path to riches.

By their believe system and lifestyle, they live at variance to anything attractive and attracting money. Wishful and hopeful thinkers. They live increasingly under the torment of the lack of money, they so love and adore, that had remained elusive to them.

Such lifestyles, could best be described as idiocies and idiotically anachronistic.

JOURNEYING TOWARDS WRECKAGE

The rich fool and poor idiots, are journeying towards wreckage in a wrecked voyage. As the former openly displays his love for money, the latter is dying from the love of money.

THE RECOMMENDED PATH

I would want to conclude with the admonition of Brother Paul;

"Godliness with contentment is great gain. For we brought nothing into this world, and it is certain we can carry nothing out. And having food and raiment let us be therewith content. But they that will be rich fall into temptation and a snare, and into many foolish and hurtful lusts, which drown men in destruction and perdition. For the love of money is the root of all evil: which while some coveted after, they have erred from the faith, and pierced themselves through with many sorrows" (1 Timothy 6:6-7).

Note, this fact; "Riches will do you no good on the day you face death, but honesty can save your life." (Proverbs 11:4).

From the staples of the lone voice crying in the wilderness.

THE MISSING GOAT NO 3

ILLUSION - THEORY OF THE MISSING GOAT

THE MISSING GOAT!?

It all started one lazy Sunday afternoon. In a small town near Toronto in Canada. Two school-going friends had a crazy idea. They rounded up three goats from the neighborhood and painted the numbers 1, 2 and 4 on their sides. That night they let the goats loose inside their school building. The next morning, when the authorities entered the school, they could smell something was wrong. They soon saw goat droppings on the stairs and near the entrance and realized that some goats had entered the building. A search was immediately launched and very soon, the three goats were found. But the authorities were worried, where was goat no. 3? They spent the rest of the day looking for goat no. 3. The school declared classes off for the students for the rest of the day. The teachers, helpers, guards, canteen staffs, boys were all busy looking for the goat no. 3, which, of course, was never found. Simply because it did not exist. Those among us who inspite of having a good life are always feeling a "lack of fulfilment" are actually looking for the elusive, missing, non-existent goat no. 3. Whatever the area of complaint or dissatisfaction, relationship, job-satisfaction, finance, achievements an absence of something is always larger than the presence of many other things. Let's stop worrying about goat no. 3 N enjoy the life...

Life would be so much happier without the worries....

HAVE A BLESSED DAY....!!!

And don't let the non-existent imaginary goat number 3 waste your time and happiness.

ENJOY LIFE WITH WHAT YOU HAVE AND WHO YOU ARE.

THE FAT (LEAN) COW

"They laid off 20 top shots today from my organization" honey pie. As I listened to her, she continued, including one highly problematic chap, thank God he got a house of his own". There and then i plunged into a ponder mode, before I knew it, I was carried away by sleep.

WASHING AND THINKING

I woke up, as usual trapped in prayers, for that has remained my routine as every other thing seemed failing. That done, I visited the car and washing and thinking, i remembered why I wrote the book, before the evil day comes - you must be prepared. I remembered I wrote, "as an employee, 5 things are likely to happen to you:

- YOU MAY BE PROMOTED

- You may be demoted
- You may resign
- You may be sacked
- You may die in the course of service"

I next admonished that "before you take up any job, be prepared for the five possibilities". So yesterday, 20 among several others were sacked. In my instance, i resigned from a fat paying job over 10 years ago and i've never looked back.

You know since i encountered that 5 possibilities, i don't get myself trapped to anyone, as the underlying would show you the dangers.

WHAT ABOUT YOU?

Are you the fat or lean cow? Which are you? And which are you romancing with or have you proposed to?
The underlying story should quicken and reawaken you. I have copied to share because of you, *so carefully read and share to whom it may concern, as it concerns you*

THE STORY BEGINS

Is there a cow in your life that is keeping you miserable?

Once upon a time, in a faraway land, there lived a Chinese wise man and his disciple. One day during their travels, they saw a hut in the distance. As they approached it, they realized that it was occupied, in spite of its extremely poor appearance.

In that desolate place where there were no crops and no trees, a man lived with his wife, three young children and a thin, tired cow. Since they were hungry and thirsty, the wise man and his disciple stopped for a few hours and were well received. At one point, the wise man asked:
"This is a very poor place, far away from anything. How do you survive?"
"You see that cow? That's what keeps us going," said the head of the family. "she gives us milk, some of it we drink and some we turn into cheese. When there is extra, we go into the city and exchange the milk and cheese for other types of food. That's how we survive."

The wise man thanked them for their hospitality and left. When he reached the first bend in the road, he said to his disciple:

"Go back, get the cow, take her to the cliff in front of us, and push her off." The disciple could not believe what he was hearing.

"I cannot do that, master! How can you be so ungrateful? The cow is all they have. If i throw it off the cliff, they will have no way of surviving. Without the cow, they will all die!"

The wise man, an elderly chinese man, took a deep breath and repeated the order:"Go ahead. Push the cow off the cliff."

Though outraged at what he was being asked to do, the disciple had to obey his master. He returned to the hut and quietly led the animal to the edge of the cliff and pushed. The cow fell down the cliff and died.

As the years passed by, remorse for what he had done never left the disciple. One spring day, the guilt became too much to bear and he left the wise man and returned to that little shack. He wanted to find out what had happened to that family, to help them out, apologize, or somehow make amends. Upon rounding a turn in the road, he could not believe what his eyes were showing him. In place of the poor shack, there was a beautiful house with trees all around, a swimming pool, several cars in the garage, a satellite dish, and more. Three good-looking teenagers and their parents were celebrating their first million dollars.

The heart of the disciple froze. What could have happened to the family? Without a doubt, they must have been starving to death and forced to sell their land and leave. At that moment, the disciple thought they must all be begging on the street corners of some city. He approached the house and asked a man that was passing by, about the whereabouts of the family that had lived there several years before.

You are looking at it," said the man, pointing to the people gathered around the barbecue. Unable to believe what he was hearing, the disciple walked through the gate and took a few steps closer to the pool where he recognized the man from several years before, only now he was strong and confident, the woman was happy, and the children were now good looking teenagers. He was dumbfounded, and went over to the man and asked:_

What happened? I was here with my teacher a few years ago and this was a miserable place. There was nothing. What did you do to improve your lives in such a short time?"

THE MAN LOOKED AT THE DISCIPLE AND REPLIED WITH A SMILE

We had a cow that kept us alive. She was all we had. But one day she fell down the cliff and died. To survive, we had to start doing other things, develop skills we didn't even know we had. And so, because we were forced to come up with new ways of doing things, we are now much better off than before.

My question is, who or what is that 'cow' in your life that you need to push off the cliff?* _many a time, we have let our dependence on certain people, things or situation, create a comfort zone and limit us from achieving greater things. Personally, I am very 'cautious' in nature and it takes me a lot to let go and climb to another level. You may feel terrible at first, but in the end, it will all be worth it.

From the conversation in the end, the man says that they had to develop skills and do other things when their only 'source of survival was dead'. At times we need to lose that job to realize that we can actually do well in business. Sometimes that business needs to fail, to realize that we can do well in other things. Sometimes a situation in our lives may have to fail for us to realize that we deserve and can get better.

Is there a cow in your life that is keeping you miserable? If so, push that cow down the cliff and please do not be tempted to go after it!

Have I talked to someone? Have you learned something?_

What's that cow that's holding you? Will you push that cow down the cliff?

From the staples of the lone voice crying in the wilderness - https://www.facebook.com/pg/a-lone-voice-crying-in-the-wilderness-2365223403711129/about/

Acknowledgement

I acknowledge GOD Almighty for granting me the enablement to publish this book. I also want to appreciate my superb husband for encouraging and supporting me throughout the writing of this book.

ABOUT THE AUTHOR

Toyosi Ade-Abass

She's a graduate of University of Ilorin (B.Sc). She's a music minister, song writer and also a preacher of the gospel. She's happily married with godly children.